D1428930

532 402 25 3

KNOW IT ALL
PLANTS

By Louise Nelson

BookLife
PUBLISHING

©2021
BookLife Publishing Ltd.
King's Lynn
Norfolk PE30 4LS

A catalogue record for this book is available from the British Library.

ISBN: 978-1-83927-459-6

All facts, statistics, web addresses and URLs in this book were verified as valid and accurate at time of writing.
No responsibility for any changes to external websites or references can be accepted by either the author or publisher.

Written by:
Louise Nelson

Edited by:
John Wood

Designed by:
Dan Scase

PHOTO CREDITS

All images are courtesy of Shutterstock.com. With thanks to Getty Images, Thinkstock Photo and iStockphoto. Front cover: Leptospira, Scisetti Alfio, Ian 2010, Dewin ID, Sergey Chirkov, Barbol, Hong Vo, Atstock Productions, pjhpix, Egor Rodynchenko, Spayder pauk_79, bergamont, Aggie 11, Ortis. 4&5 – jocic, davooda, Teerasak, JIANG HONGYAN, Masyanya, 3dmentor, Wichai Prasomsri1, HedvikaMichnova.jpg, Guliveris, Ailisa. 6&7 – Indypendenz, Tridsanu Thopet, A3pfamily, Binh Thanh Bui, Dean Drobot, Wisiel, Photoongraphy. 8&9 – Master1305, Krakenimages.com, nevodka, Smit, shipfactory, Lepas, Ryan M. Bolton, MANDY GODBEHEAR, Kuttelvaserova Stuchelova, Dr. Norbert Lange, Tony Bierman, NOPPHARAT6395. 10&11 – Vahe 3D, arka38, Andrii Antonov, Neo Tribbiani, Holiday.Photo.Top, Nerthuz, Delbars, Vasin Lee, Andrew b Stowe. 12&13 – Valentina Razumova, Christopher Bailey, milart, Nerthuz, kpboonjit, Alena Brozova, Marynka Mandarinka, Serg64, Daomanee. 14&15 – nulinukas, Emily Li, Roman Samokhin, SeDmi, Tim UR, P Kyriakos, Ihor Hvozdetskyi, Boonchuay1970, Boonchuay1970, JIANG HONGYAN, Abel Tumik, L. Feddes, Toong Stockers, Maks Narodenko. 16&17 – Alena Brozova, Spalnic, EM Arts, Anna Kucherova, Tim UR, yadom, Emilio100, Elena Koromyslova, Krasowit. 18&19 – Reha Mark, Casther, anat chant, Ruth Black, AnnaKT, Ammak, nopporn0510, Richard Griffin, Valery121283, AjayTvm. 20&21 – natthawut ngoensanthia, Alf Ribeiro, Mikhail Ivannikov, Hathaikorn, jeep2499, TamuT, deckorator, TRMK. 22&23 – Anton Starikov, Elena Schweitzer, NIPAPORN PANYACHAROEN, angnokever, Sodel Vladyslav, Mariusz S. Jurgielewicz, Le Do, Vladimir Konstantinov, Elena Butinova, Mny-Jhee, Lightspring, Tetiana Rostopira. 24&25 – Andrew E Gardner, mervin07, ilikestudio, Darren Kurnia, Africa Studio, Anastasiya Yacenko. 26&27 – Roman Samokhin, Yasonya, Anna Kucherova, TopFotography, grey_and, Nattika, Viktor Loki, Wang LiQiang, EVGEIIA. 28&29 – Linda Macpherson, Krasowit, Jirik V, Richard Griffin, Richard Griffin. 30&31 – Ratthaphong Ekariyasap, Anna Sedneva, kuzina, ninoninos, Valentyn Volkov, ZaZa Studio, Gerrit Bunt, pukach, kirillov alexey, Iryna Kalamurza. 32&33 – Sharlotta, Eskymaks, Ivonne Wierink, Faizal Ramli, Gts, Hong Vo, Flower Studio, Algirdas Gelazius. 34&35 – LiuSol, studiovin, Wachiraphorn Thongya, Anton Starikov, Atjanan Charoensiri, Rawpixel.com, Shebeko. 36&37 – Olga Danylenko, Rybnikova Olga.

CONTENTS

Words that look like this can be found in the glossary on page 38.
Key ideas you will need can be found on page 6.

THE GRASS IS GREENER

There's grass in the garden, trees in the woods and maybe even flowers outside your window. There are plants everywhere! This is a good thing because plants are very important to life on Earth. They clean our air, give us food, and much more. But what are they, exactly?

ROSE

CACTUS

POTATO

SEAWEED

GRASS

FERN

There are around 390,000 types of plant – and that's just the ones we know about! New types of plant are being found all the time.

A plant is a living thing. Plants grow in soil, water or on another plant. Plants usually have a stem, leaves and roots. Most of them have flowers and seeds. All the pictures on these two pages are of plants. How many more can you think of?

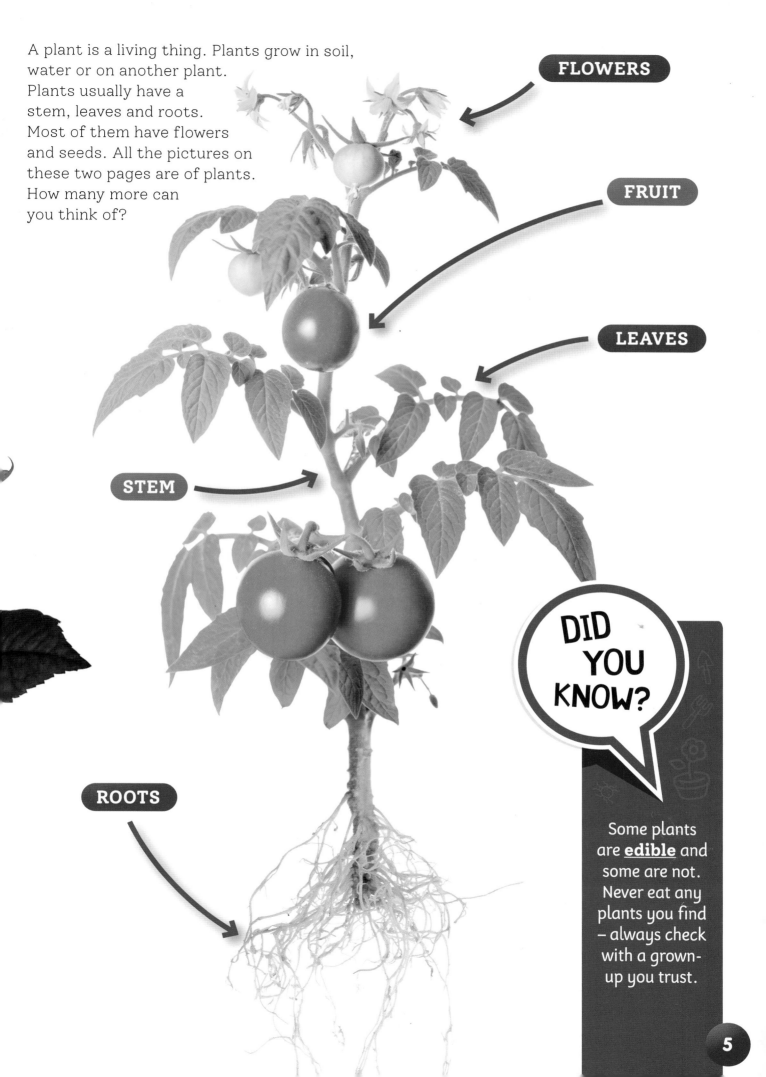

FLOWERS

FRUIT

LEAVES

STEM

ROOTS

DID YOU KNOW?

Some plants are **edible** and some are not. Never eat any plants you find – always check with a grown-up you trust.

KEY IDEAS

Growing is when a living thing changes and becomes bigger. All plants and animals grow.

Plants grow from tiny seeds...

... to mighty trees!

PHOTOSYNTHESIS

Photosynthesis is how plants make food. Plants take in sunlight to make food. This happens in special parts of the plant, which have lots of chlorophyll. Chlorophyll helps them turn sunlight into food. Chlorophyll is also what gives plants a green colour.

Eat your greens!

Kale leaves are dark green. They contain a lot of chlorophyll.

FRUIT AND VEGETABLES

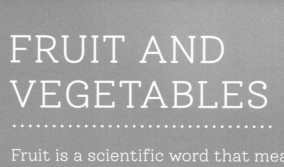

Fruit is a scientific word that means the part of the plant that holds the seeds. But when we talk about plants we eat, fruits mean sweet-tasting plant parts, and vegetables means **savoury**-tasting plant parts.

Tomatoes are a fruit to scientists, and a vegetable to chefs!

VEGETABLE

FRUIT

WHAT ARE PLANTS?

A plant is a living thing. There are seven **characteristics** that all living things have. This is true for every single living thing, from you to a potato. Let's look closely at them here.

Living things can take in and give out air.

Living things can move on their own.

Living things can **sense** the world around them.

Living things need food.

Living things **reproduce**.

Living things grow.

Living things get rid of their **waste**.

Plants share all of these characteristics with animals. Animals and plants are more like each other than you might think.

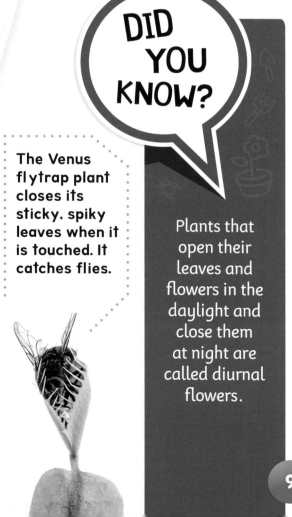

The moonflower opens its flowers at night. It is <u>nocturnal</u>.

Some plants open and close their leaves and flowers.

You might not think it, but plants do move – just very slowly. Plants that have flowers often follow the Sun as it rises, passes overhead and sets. Plants also grow towards light.

Some types of <u>algae</u> can move towards light!

The Venus flytrap plant closes its sticky, spiky leaves when it is touched. It catches flies.

DID YOU KNOW?

Plants that open their leaves and flowers in the daylight and close them at night are called diurnal flowers.

WHAT PLANTS NEED

Plants start off small, then grow to their full size. In order to live well and grow, plants need certain things. Let's see what they are:

Plants need water for photosynthesis, to help take in _nutrients_ and to keep itself healthy.

Plants need light to make food. Plants take in light, then make their own food. This is called photosynthesis.

Plants need the right _temperature_. Some plants need hot, bright sunshine. Others need cooler air.

Plants need clean air to grow well. Dirty or _polluted_ air is bad for plants.

Plants need nutrients. They use these with light to make food. Soil and _fertiliser_ have a lot of nutrients.

Just like animals, plants need the right habitat to live in. A habitat is the place a living thing can grow and **thrive**, because it has all the things the living thing needs. A plant's habitat must have the right temperature, food, water and space. Different plants need different habitats.

These pine trees grow in a cold habitat.

Water lilies grow in **fresh water**.

Kelp is a plant that grows in huge underwater forests.

DID YOU KNOW?

Some plants can even grow in the hot, dry desert.

PARTS OF A PLANT

There are thousands of different types of plants. They are all very different, but they all have a few things **in common**. The main parts of most plants are the roots, leaves and stem.

Here are some examples of different plant parts:

FLOWER

Flowers **attract** bees and other insects to the plant to help it spread its pollen (find out more on page 24).

LEAF

Leaves take in sunlight and use it to make food for the plant.

SEED

New plants grow from seeds.

STEM

The stem is the part of the plant above the ground. It **supports** the plant, and carries water and nutrients to the rest of the plant.

ROOT

The roots are below the ground. They hold the plant in place, and take in water and nutrients from the soil.

AVOCADO SEEDS

PUMPKIN SEEDS

Cactus stems are spiky.

Leaves can be big... or tiny!

Tree trunks are stems too!

Bright, colourful flowers attract bees.

This seedling has already put out roots (find out about seedlings on page 16).

13

PLANTS **WITH** SEEDS

Flowering plants and **conifers** have seeds. These plants make seeds to make more of themselves. Trees, grasses and bushes can all be flowering plants. Many plants with seeds also make fruit. Flowers can be big, bright and colourful, or very tiny.

The spiky fruit of the horse chestnut tree hides a seed inside... a conker!

This is a tomato flower. The fruit grows from the centre of the flower. The seeds are inside.

SEEDS

Conifers make cones which hold their seeds.

Sunflower seeds are found in the middle of the large, flowering head.

Apples grow on apple trees. The seeds can be found inside the fruit.

These are
moss spores.

These are spores on a fern leaf.

PLANTS **WITHOUT** SEEDS

Ferns and mosses do not make flowers or seeds. They make spores instead. Spores are tiny **cells** that make a new plant.

SAFE TO EAT?

Monkshood plants are beautiful... but deadly! Every part of the plant can kill you.

Some plants are safe – and tasty – to eat. Some plants have parts that can be eaten, such as the root or the fruit. Other plants are not edible. They can even be poisonous.

These plant parts are safe to eat:

KIWI
FRUIT

DID
YOU
KNOW?

ASPARAGUS
STEMS

SUNFLOWER
SEEDS

Just four nightshade berries are enough to kill you. Could you tell them apart from these tasty blackcurrants?

SEEDS AND BULBS

Most flowering plants grow from either seeds or bulbs. Seeds are small parts of a plant. New plants grow from seeds. Seeds need the right temperature, soil and amount of water to grow.

SEEDLING

RADICLE

SEED

Seeds contain all the food the new baby plant needs to grow.

Seeds put out a tiny root. called a radicle. then a small shoot. called a seedling.

Sweetcorn is a type of seed.

Beans are a type of seed.

Tree nuts are also a type of seed. Nuts are seeds with hard shells.

Stones (also called pits) inside fruits are seeds too.

Seeds are tiny living things. but they are <u>dormant</u> until they have everything they need to grow.

BULBS

Bulbs are an **organ** that stores food for the plant. They have fleshy leaves. Bulbs can grow into a new plant, which will be exactly the same as the parent plant.

Beautiful crocus flowers grow from bulbs.

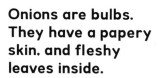

Onions are bulbs. They have a papery skin. and fleshy leaves inside.

This tuber will grow into a begonia.

Tubers are another organ that stores food for plants. Tubers grow underground, and like bulbs they can grow into a new plant.

Potatoes are tubers.

ROOTS AND STEMS

ROOTS

Roots are like branches underneath the ground. Roots have two jobs. Firstly, they hold the plant in place. The deeper the roots go, the harder it will be for the plant to come out of the ground. Secondly, they work like drinking straws, sucking up nutrients and water for the plant.

Tree roots almost look like another upside-down, underground tree! Tree roots can be very deep.

Carrots are the roots of the plant. Roots we eat are called root vegetables.

Ginger is a type of root. Ginger is used to make gingerbread.

STEMS

Some long stems, also known as vines, can climb walls and surfaces.

Stems are the strong plant parts that hold the leaves and flowers up. They also take nutrients and water from the roots and carry them to the leaves and flowers. Stems are full of tiny plant parts that are like tubes.

The red food colouring here shows where the tubes run up this stem of celery. The plant has sucked the red water up the tubes.

This yellow gorse has thorns on its stem. Thorns are short, spiky stems. They protect the plant.

Cinnamon is a **spice** made of bark from a tree trunk.

DID YOU KNOW?

Plant stems have many different uses. Branches and tree trunks are used to build things. Plant stems can make food and paper. We can weave them into baskets and clothes. Amazing!

Plants that climb often have tendrils. These are special curly stems that wrap around things as they grow.

TENDRIL

The stem of a tree is its trunk.

CASE STUDY: BANANAS

Banana plants

Do you like bananas? Bananas are delicious and healthy for you too. Bananas are actually a berry, which is a type of fruit. Berries have their seeds buried inside the fleshy part. Banana plants can grow to around seven metres tall. The leaves of the banana plant can be almost three metres long.

The bananas grow in the heat of the Sun. They are green and grow fast.

This is a banana flower being visited by a monarch butterfly. Can you see the tiny bananas?

When the flower has fallen away, the bananas are green. They are not **ripe** yet.

The banana plants keep growing...

... and growing!

All of these bananas grew from a single stem!

Bananas are a popular food all over the world. Most bananas are grown in India, China and the Philippines. Banana plants need good soil, lots of water, and warm temperatures to grow.

FACT FILE: BANANAS

- Banana plants are not trees, even if they look like it. Their stems have no wood, so they are a herb!

- A single banana is a finger, and a cluster of them together is sometimes called a hand. Can you guess why?

- Bananas make a great snack before sports or exercise.

In colder countries, such as the UK, banana plants can grow indoors. However, these plants will probably not make any fruit.

21

LEAVES

Leaves take in **carbon dioxide** from the air, light from the Sun and water through the roots and stem. Through photosynthesis, they turn these things into food. The plant can use this food to give it energy.

The leaves of a pine tree are long, thin and sharp. They are called needles.

Eucalyptus leaves have a strong, fresh smell. Oil made from these leaves is used in cold and flu medicine to help clear your nose.

Lettuce leaves are delicious!

Clover usually has three heart-shaped leaves. It is considered very lucky to find a four-leaf clover.

Duckweed leaves are tiny. They are less than one-half of a centimetre across!

Amazon water lilies are a type of water lily. Their enormous flat leaves can grow to over two-and-a-half metres across.

Amazon water lily leaves are strong enough to hold the weight of a small child.

Trees can be split into two groups. Evergreen plants have green leaves all year round. Dead leaves drop off and are replaced slowly. Deciduous plants are the opposite. Their leaves change colour as the seasons change, falling off in the autumn and growing back all at once in the spring.

Oak leaves are green in the spring. In the autumn, they turn golden brown and fall off. The seeds of oak trees are called acorns.

Fir trees are evergreen. Their slim needles have a waxy coating which protects them from the cold and keeps the water inside.

Autumn is a colourful time. Leaves can turn the trees from green to orange, brown, yellow, gold and copper.

DID YOU KNOW?

Christmas trees are evergreen – but many still drop their needle-shaped leaves all over the floor once they aren't in the ground anymore!

Leaves of deciduous trees are broad and flat compared to the thin needles of pines and conifers. This means the tree can make lots and lots of food all summer – enough to last through the winter when it can't make any more.

FLOWERS

There are many different types of flower. They come in all sorts of colours and shapes – and with different smells! Flowers might all look different, but they've actually got a lot in common. While they seem different, they all have the same basic parts.

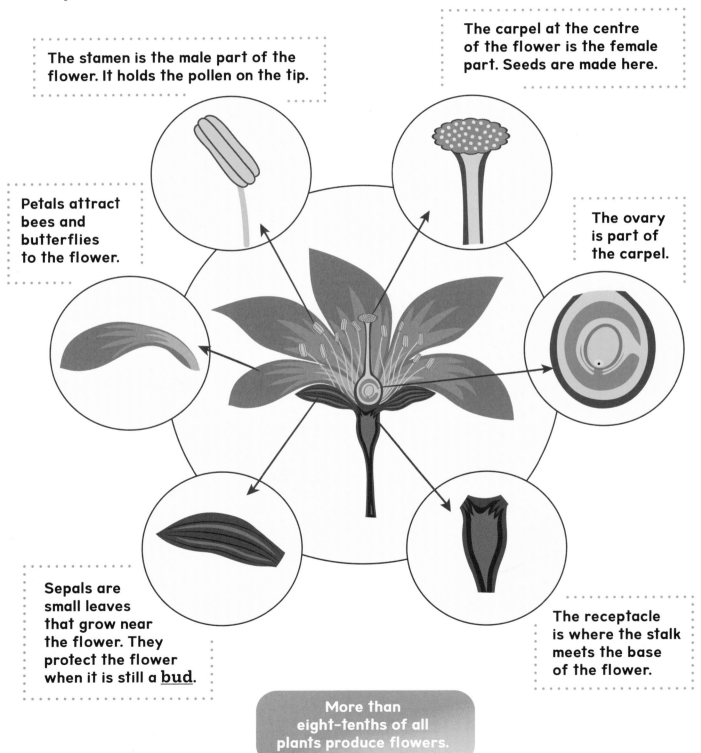

The stamen is the male part of the flower. It holds the pollen on the tip.

The carpel at the centre of the flower is the female part. Seeds are made here.

Petals attract bees and butterflies to the flower.

The ovary is part of the carpel.

Sepals are small leaves that grow near the flower. They protect the flower when it is still a <u>bud</u>.

The receptacle is where the stalk meets the base of the flower.

More than eight-tenths of all plants produce flowers.

Flowers need to attract bees and other insects so they can be pollinated. Pollination is when bees or other insects pick up the pollen and carry it to another part of the flower, or to a different flower. When the pollen has been given to a new plant, that plant can make seeds.

This bee has pollen all over its furry body.

Butterflies also pollinate flowers. The pollen sticks to the butterfly's body.

If you look very closely at the centre of a sunflower, you will see that it isn't one flower – it's hundreds! Each tiny bell in the middle of the sunflower head is a single, tiny flower.

Some people are <u>allergic</u> to the pollen from flowers. This is commonly known as hay fever.

DID YOU KNOW?

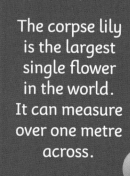

This is the corpse lily. It <u>blooms</u> only for a few days, and smells like rotten meat. This smell attracts flies and insects.

The corpse lily is the largest single flower in the world. It can measure over one metre across.

FRUIT

The fruit is the part of a plant that has the seeds in. Fruit can be fleshy, like a berry or an apple. It can also be dry, like a nut. Seeds are found inside the fruit. Fruit falls off the plant and falls to the ground. On the ground it **rots** away, leaving the seeds in the soil.

Kiwi fruit has tiny seeds.

Mango stones are seeds.

Cucumbers are fruits. Can you see the seeds inside?

There are lots of seeds inside this pumpkin.

Pomegranate seeds are covered in sweet jelly.

Have you ever eaten watermelon seeds?

26

Birds eat berries and fruit. The seeds come out in their droppings. Birds can spread seeds a long way.

The brown bear who left this behind must have eaten a lot of cherries... look at all those seeds!

Some fruits are eaten by animals. Animals eat the flesh of the fruit and then poo out the seeds, which can grow into new plants. When the animal moves around, the seeds are spread around a larger area.

This monkey is eating a banana.

DID YOU KNOW?

Seeds must be spread far away so they don't take each other's water, sunlight or nutrients. Too many plants in a small area would mean most of them would die.

Potato plants put out a small fruit that looks like a tomato – but don't eat them! They are very poisonous.

THE LIFE CYCLE OF A PLANT

All living things have a life cycle. They are born, they grow and change, and then they reach **maturity**. Living things make more of themselves. Plants mostly do this with seeds, spores or tubers. At the end of the life cycle, the living thing dies, and the life cycle is complete. Here is an example of the life cycle of some plants.

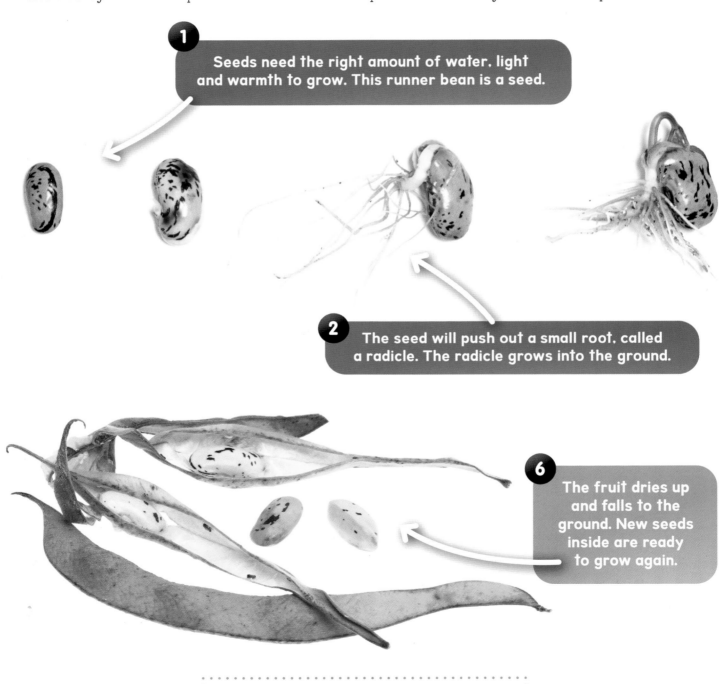

1 Seeds need the right amount of water, light and warmth to grow. This runner bean is a seed.

2 The seed will push out a small root, called a radicle. The radicle grows into the ground.

6 The fruit dries up and falls to the ground. New seeds inside are ready to grow again.

Some plants grow, make seeds and die. Others can make seeds year after year.

3 The seed then pushes out a shoot. This is a small stem with two leaves at the top.

The seedling grows with the right amounts of light, water and nutrients. New leaves grow. **4**

DID YOU KNOW?

Beans are a very important crop. Crops are plants that humans grow lots of, usually for food.

5 The plant is fully grown. It grows bright flowers to attract insects. When it has been pollinated, it will form fruit.

PLANTS AND PEOPLE

Plants are very important to people, and to all life on Earth. People use plants for shelter, food, water, medicine and clothing. New ways of using plants are being found all the time.

We build houses out of wood. Wood comes from the trunks of trees.

Fruits and vegetables are delicious and healthy.

Cucumbers are over nine-tenths water.

Soya beans are a very important crop.

Plants found in rainforests are very important for making medicine.

Cotton is used to make fabric, such as this t-shirt.

Plants take in carbon dioxide from the air and put out oxygen. Humans breathe in oxygen and breathe out carbon dioxide. This means that plants clean the air for us, making it safe to breathe again.

Rope is often made from a plant called jute.

Rubber is made of the <u>sap</u> from trees. It is soft and stretchy.

Flowers such as jasmine are used to make perfumes.

DID YOU KNOW?

There are over 20,000 types of edible plant.

Having plants in your home helps keep the air fresh.

BELIEVE IT OR NOT!

The world's tallest Christmas tree was 67.36 metres tall. It was put outside the Northgate Shopping Centre in Seattle, US, in December, 1950.

In Holland in the 1600s, tulip bulbs were worth a huge amount of money. This was known as tulip mania.

Ginkgo biloba is a very ancient type of plant. **Fossils** of ginkgo biloba leaves have been found that are 220 million years old!

Saffron is a spice. The red threads are collected from crocus flowers and are used to colour food yellow.

Peanuts are not nuts. They grow in a pod, and so they are actually a <u>legume</u>.

The baobab tree is found in Africa. It can store thousands of litres of water in its trunk.

The castor bean plant is the most poisonous common plant in the world. The beans contain a <u>toxin</u> called ricin.

Amber is hardened sap from a tree. Millions of years ago, if insects were trapped in the sticky sap, they never rotted away. This means we can now see them exactly how they looked all those years ago.

ACTIVITIES

Can you complete these fun activities?

COLOUR ME BEAUTIFUL

You can see how stems take up water with a simple experiment. You will need:

WATER

FOOD DYE

VASES OR JARS

WHITE CUT FLOWERS

Fill a different jar with water for each colour, then add a few drops of food dye to each one, keeping the colours separate. Add a white flower to each jar. Over a few days, you should see the dye appear in the white petals, colouring your flowers!

HOT OFF THE PRESS

If you put flowers and leaves between the pages of a book, then pile heavy books on top, you can press all the water out of them. The beautiful, pressed flowers left behind will have no water in them, so they won't rot. Pressed flowers can be used in your favourite crafting.

Pressed flowers can be used to record flowers you have found in a notebook.

QUICK QUIZZES

Can you remember the answers to all these questions? Check back through the book if you aren't sure.

1. What does the Venus flytrap plant eat?

a) Sugar

b) Flies

c) Sunlight

2. What do we call plants that open their leaves and flowers in the day and close at night?

a) Diurnal

b) Nocturnal

c) Dimorphic

3. What are leaves used for?

a) Food

b) Protection

c) Attracting insects

4. What is the stem of a tree also called?

a) Trunk

b) Stalk

c) Whip

5. What is the name of the seed of the horse chestnut tree?

a) Acorn

b) Conker

c) Chestnut

6. Where do tubers grow?

a) Underground

b) Above ground

c) At the base of the flower

7. What part of a plant is the stone inside a peach?

a) Fruit

b) Stem

c) Seed

8. Which type of tree loses its leaves in the autumn?

a) Evergreen

b) Diurnal

c) Deciduous

9. What is special about the corpse lily?

a) It smells like chocolate

b) It smells like rotten meat

c) It smells like cheese

10. Which part of the tulip plant was worth lots of money in 1600s Holland?

a) Bulb

b) Stem

c) Leaf

11. What is the world's most poisonous common plant?

a) Runner bean

b) Castor bean

c) Baked bean

12. What are peanuts?

a) Nuts

b) Legumes

c) Flowers

GLOSSARY

A

algae a plant or plant-like living thing that has no roots, stems, leaves or flowers

allergic getting feelings of illness from something such as nuts

attract pull or lure something in

B

blooms when a plant creates flowers

bud a small growth on a plant that develops into a leaf, flower or shoot

C

carbon dioxide a natural gas that is found in the air that humans breathe out

cells the basic building blocks that, when put together, make up all living things

characteristics features of a living thing that help to identify it

conifers a bush or tree that produces cones and usually has leaves that are green all year

D

dormant not active or growing, but ready to grow later

E

edible safe to be eaten

F

fertiliser something put on soil to help it grow certain plants

fossils parts of plants and animals from a long time ago that have been kept in good condition inside rocks

fresh water water that is not salty

I

in common having things that are the same or alike

L

legume a type of food that includes peas, peanuts, lentils and beans

M

maturity the point at which something is fully grown and able to reproduce

N

nocturnal active at night instead of during the day

nutrients natural things found in food and drink that plants and animals need to grow and stay healthy

O

organ a part of a living thing that has a specific, important job

P

polluted made harmful or dirty through the actions of humans

R

reproduce have children or make more of something

ripe when a fruit is ready to be eaten

rots breaks down

S

sap a sticky juice made by a plant

savoury one of the main types of taste; savoury foods include pasta, nuts and meat

sense to feel or be aware of

spice a plant part that has been crushed or chopped, which is added to food to give it flavour

supports holds up

T

temperature how hot or cold something is

thrive do well

toxin something poisonous which is produced by plants or animals

tree nuts nuts that come from trees, such as almonds, Brazil nuts and cashews

W

waste things left over that are no longer needed

INDEX